Life As ...

Life As a Pioneer on the Oregon Trail

Jeri Freedman

Cavendish Square

New York

Published in 2016 by Cavendish Square Publishing, LLC
243 5th Avenue, Suite 136, New York, NY 10016

First Edition

Website: cavendishsq.com

This publication represents the opinions and views of the author based on his or her personal experience, knowledge,
and research. The information in this book serves as a general guide only. The author and publisher have used their best
efforts in preparing this book and disclaim liability rising directly or indirectly from the use and application of this book.

CPSIA Compliance Information: Batch #CW16CSQ

All websites were available and accurate when this book was sent to press.

Cataloging-in-Publication Data

Freedman, Jeri.
Life as a pioneer on the Oregon Trail / by Jeri Freedman.
p. cm. — (Life as)
Includes index.
ISBN 978-1-5026-1076-8 (hardcover) ISBN 978-1-5026-1075-1 (paperback) ISBN 978-1-5026-1077-5 (ebook)
1. Pioneers — Oregon National Historic Trail — History — Juvenile literature.
2. Pioneers — Oregon National Historic Trail — Social life and customs — Juvenile literature.
3. Frontier and pioneer life — Oregon National Historic Trail — Juvenile literature. I. Freedman, Jeri. II. Title.
F597.F74 2016
978'.02—d23

Editorial Director: David McNamara
Editor: Kristen Susienka
Copy Editor: Nathan Heidelberger
Art Director: Jeff Talbot
Designer: Joe Macri
Senior Production Manager: Jennifer Ryder-Talbot
Production Editor: Renni Johnson
Photo Research: J8 Media

The photographs in this book are used by permission and through the courtesy of: FPG/Getty Images, cover; Marco
Mayer/Shutterstock, cover (and throughout the book); Victorian Traditions/Shutterstock, 5; Peter Newark American
Pictures/Bridgeman Images, 6; Universal Images Group/Getty Images, 9; Archive Holdings Inc./Getty Images, 10; Oregon
Historical Society, 13; Jon Bilous/Shutterstock, 15; Didecs/Shutterstock, 16; Library of Congress, 17; Donna Beeler/
Shutterstock, 19, Science Source/Getty Images, 20; Dmbaker/Thinkstock, 21; Tracy Whiteside/Thinkstock, 23;
Eon Images, JRL Photographer/Thinkstock, 24; Library of Congress, 25; Josemaria Toscano/Shutterstock, 27.

Printed in the United States of America

Contents

Introduction

Imagine leaving your home, saying good-bye to your friends, getting in a covered wagon with your family, and riding far away to a place you've never seen. People called pioneers did that in the 1800s. Pioneers were people who wished to live in the western United States. There they could get land to start farms. Going west, pioneers had to cross large fields called **plains** and go over the Rocky Mountains. Many pioneers followed the Oregon Trail, a 2,200-mile (3,500-kilometer) route from the **Midwest** to Oregon. Along the way, they faced many dangers.

Families traveled across the plains to a new home in Oregon.

This map shows the paths of the Oregon Trail.

Chapter 1
History of the Oregon Trail

The Oregon Trail started as separate trails used by Native Americans. In the early 1800s, fur traders used the trails to create one path. This path joined places where traders could sell animal furs. Christians sent people along the trail in the 1830s to get the Native Americans to believe in Christianity. In the early 1840s, newspapers began to publish stories of how wonderful Oregon was. People in eastern cities began to head west. Some wanted land to farm. Others were runaway slaves. They would be free if they could get to Oregon.

The first group of pioneers to travel the Oregon Trail left Independence, Missouri, in 1841. They followed the fur traders' route. They took an easy mountain pass in Wyoming through the Rocky Mountains. Finally, they reached Oregon. Afterward, thousands of people traveled the Oregon Trail. By 1884, railroads connected Oregon to the rest of the United States. After that, people no longer traveled the trail by wagon.

The Gold Rush

In 1848, gold was discovered in California. This discovery started the Gold Rush. Many people hoped to get rich from the gold in California. They traveled the Oregon Trail to get there. The first people who came looking for gold were single men. Men with families came later. People set up businesses to serve the men and their families. Not everyone became rich. Gold was not always easy to find.

Finding gold was hard work for gold miners.

Many people who traveled the Oregon Trail used wagons.

Chapter 2
Being a Pioneer

In the 1800s, many families living on the East Coast decided to go west to find cheap or free land. Oregon was a new **territory** and many people wanted to live there. In Oregon, people could build a house and have a farm. They could not do that in a busy East Coast city.

In May 1843, a large group of wagons, called a **wagon train**, left Missouri and traveled to Oregon. The wagon train had 120 wagons, about 1,000 people, and 5,000 cattle. The wagons were different sizes. One kind of wagon was the Conestoga wagon. It had lots of room to carry belongings. Pioneers packed food and clothing for the entire trip. **Settlers** brought lots of biscuits, bacon, coffee, tea, sugar, beans, rice, dried fruit, and dried meat. They also brought seeds to plant crops such as wheat, corn, and vegetables. Large furniture was too heavy to take. Instead they sent it by ship to the West Coast.

Oregon Trail Facts

About five hundred thousand people traveled the Oregon Trail. It cost $100 to $200 (about $2,200 to $4,500 in 2015) and took five to six months. The trail crossed parts of Kansas, Nebraska, Wyoming, Idaho, and Oregon.

The pioneers traveled across grassy plains. It was hot during the day and cold at night. There were often storms. They had to cross the Rocky Mountains. The highest parts of the mountains were covered with snow. On the other side, they had to cross deserts and forests. It was not an easy journey.

Dr. Elijah White

Elijah White was a doctor and a **missionary**. Missionaries wanted to teach Native Americans about religion. In 1843, he led the first large wagon train along the Oregon Trail.

Pioneers crossed rivers such as the Columbia River (pictured here) to get to Oregon.

Chapter 3

Life on the Trail

A pioneer's life on the trail began early and ended late. Once awake, men began to take down tents and round up cattle. Women and children cooked food such as **porridge** and bacon for breakfast. After breakfast, men hitched oxen or mules to the wagons. Women washed and put away dishes and pots. Then the wagons began to travel.

Unless they were sick or crossing difficult parts of the trail, most people walked. Riding in wagons was uncomfortable. Riding also made the wagons heavier, since wagons carried supplies. Some people rode horses.

Around noon, they would stop to rest and eat lunch. Typically, a group traveled 15 to 20 miles

(24 to 32 km) a day. Around 5 p.m., the leaders of the wagon train would look for a good place to set up camp. Families would then eat dinner and do chores, such as taking care of animals and fixing clothes. They would play music and dance. Everyone went to sleep by 8 p.m. Men would take turns throughout the night guarding the people and animals.

Daily Schedule of a Pioneer

A pioneer's day might go like this:

4 a.m.	Wake up
5 a.m.	Eat breakfast
7 a.m.	Start traveling on the trail
12 p.m.	Stop to eat lunch
1 p.m.	Travel again
5 p.m.	Set up camp for the night
6 p.m.	Eat dinner
7 p.m.	Do chores
8 p.m.	Go to bed

A wagon train crosses a river.

Pioneers faced many dangers. Sometimes people were attacked by Native Americans. Other times, people were hurt or killed in accidents with guns or by falling from horses or mules. Sometimes people drowned while crossing rivers. On steep parts of the trail, wagons could overturn and hurt people. Bad weather was another problem.

Children on the Trail

Many children traveled with their parents. They had to leave their friends and other family members behind. There wasn't room in the wagon for many toys, so they had to leave most of them behind, too. Many children were worried, sad, or scared.

On the trail, children had chores. They fetched water and collected materials to make fires at night. Children herded animals and milked cows. They also helped with cooking and cleaning. In the evening there was time for playing, singing, and dancing.

Children often traveled with their parents to a new home in the West.

Four to six oxen were used to pull a wagon.

Chapter 4

Tools for Pioneers

Animals pulled the wagons. Mules and oxen were most common. They were strong and could survive by eating grass. Oxen were the best choice. They could survive the journey, and they were much better than mules at traveling over rough areas and crossing streams. They were stronger than mules and could pull a lot of weight. This helped if a wagon got stuck in mud. A person called a driver guided the animals and walked next to them.

Buffalo were commonly seen roaming the plains.

The most important tool on the trail was the wagon. It was often covered to keep away dust and bugs and to give people shade. The bed of the covered wagon was 9 to 11 feet (2.7 to 3.4 meters) long. It was about 4 feet (1.2 m) wide and 10 feet (3 m) tall. The top of the wagon was made of canvas. The canvas was covered with paint or special oil to make it waterproof. It had big wooden wheels that could go over bumps easily. These wagons were nicknamed prairie schooners because their big white tops looked like the sails of a type of sailing ship called a schooner.

Rifles

Weapons were important, and settlers usually carried guns called rifles. With rifles, the pioneers could protect themselves and their belongings from attackers and thieves. More importantly, pioneers used rifles to hunt for food. Animals such as buffalo gave them fresh meat.

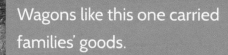

Wagons like this one carried families' goods.

Pioneers made their wagons into rafts to cross rivers.

Pioneers brought tools with them so they could farm and build houses in Oregon. These tools included shovels, rakes, saws, plows, axes, and hammers. Tools like shovels and rakes were also used by men who walked ahead of the wagon train. They cleared the trail of rocks and bushes so the wagons would not run over them. Pioneers also used their tools to repair wagons. Wheels and other parts of a wagon sometimes broke when going over rough ground or across streams.

The wagon wheels had iron rims to protect them.

Chapter 5

Settling the West

In the 1800s, most people in the United States lived on the East Coast or in the Midwest. Many Americans believed that the United States should control the western part of the continent as well. This idea was called **manifest destiny**. It was one reason pioneers wanted to move to the West. The Oregon Trail was the main path from the East and Midwest

In the West, pioneers built log houses.

to the Oregon Territory, which included what is now Oregon, Washington state, Idaho, and parts of Wyoming and Montana.

Originally, the Oregon Territory was claimed by both Great Britain and the United States. American pioneers settling the Oregon Territory helped make it part of the United States. By the late 1800s, America stretched from the Atlantic Ocean to the Pacific Ocean. The Oregon Trail also let large numbers of people go to California during the Gold Rush. These people settled California. Without the Oregon Trail, states such as Idaho, Washington, Oregon, and California might not be part of the United States today.

Cities in Oregon exist today because of the pioneers who settled them.

Glossary

manifest destiny The belief that Americans were meant to settle the continent from coast to coast.

Midwest The part of the United States that is around the Mississippi River.

missionary A member of a church who travels to get other people to join the religion.

plains Land covered with tall grass and very few trees.

porridge Grain, such as oatmeal, boiled with water or milk.

settlers People who set up a new community in a part of a country.

territory An area of land that belongs to a country but is not officially a state.

wagon train A long string of wagons traveling together.

Find Out More

Books

Doeden, Matt. *The Oregon Trail: An Interactive History Adventure*. North Mankato, MN: Capstone Press, 2013.

Friedman, Mel. *The Oregon Trail*. New York: Children's Press, 2010.

Gregory, Christiana. *Across the Wide and Lonesome Prairie: The Oregon Trail Diary of Hattie Campbell, 1847*. New York: Scholastic Press, 2012.

Website

Oregon Trail for Kids

www.ducksters.com/history/westward_expansion/oregon_trail.php

Video

In Pursuit of a Dream (DVD). The Oregon-California Trails Association, 2009.

Index

Page numbers in **boldface** are illustrations. Entries in **boldface** are glossary terms.

territory, 11, 26

wagon, 4, 8, **10**, 11, 15, 18, **20**, 21–22, **23**, 24
    Conestoga wagon, 11
    dimensions of, 22

prairie schooner, 22
    wheels of, 22, **24**

wagon train, 11, 13, 16, **17**, 24

White, Elijah, 13, **13**

About the Author

Jeri Freedman has a Bachelor of Arts degree from Harvard University. She is the author of more than forty children's and young adult nonfiction books, including *Massachusetts: Past and Present, Louisiana: Past and Present, Iowa: Past and Present*, and *The Warsaw Ghetto and Uprising*. She is also the coauthor of two alternate history science fiction novels published under the name Ellen Foxxe.